Everything You Need To Know About

TEEN

PREGNANCY

Many young women become pregnant when they are in their teens.

Everything You Need To Know About
TEEN
PREGNANCY

Tracy Hughes

Series Editor: Evan Stark, Ph.D.

THE ROSEN PUBLISHING GROUP, INC.
NEW YORK

Lourdes High School Library
4034 West 56th Street
Chicago, Illinois 60629

Published in 1988 by The Rosen Publishing Group, Inc
29 East 21st Street, New York City, New York 10010

Second printing
Copyright 1988 by The Rosen Publishing Group, Inc

90 -17279

All rights reserved. No part of this book may be
reproduced in any form without permission in writing
from the publisher, except by a reviewer.

Manufactured in the United States of America

53095

Library of Congress Cataloging-in-Publication Data

Hughes, Tracy.
    Everything you need to know about teen pregnancy.
    (The Need to know library)
    Summary: Discusses such aspects of teenage pregnancy
as the causes and nature of pregnancy, the proper care
for mother and baby, and alternative choices such as
adoption and abortion.
    Bibliography: p. 62
    Includes index.
    1. Teenage pregnancy—United States—Juvenile
literature. [1. Pregnancy. 2. Sex instruction for
youth] I. Title.   II. Series.
HQ759.4.H84   1988   618.2'024042   88-26367
ISBN 0-8239-0810-0

618.2
HUG

Contents

Introduction

For a teenager, an unplanned pregnancy is a tough thing to deal with. It is tough even for an adult woman. An unexpected pregnancy means that many hard choices must be made. The situation is even harder for a teenager.

Most teenage girls become pregnant by accident. Often it is because they do not know the facts about pregnancy. They do not know how pregnancy occurs. Many teenage girls do not know the facts about birth control either. They don't learn because they are too embarrassed. They don't want to talk about sex. But without these facts it is easy to become pregnant by accident.

Often a pregnant teen feels very alone. She feels like the only one in the world who has this problem. But more than a million young women become pregnant each year.

What should you do when you accidently become pregnant? The best first step is to go to someone you trust. Talk to a person who will give you support and advice. Then you can see what choices you have. You can also think about which choices are right for you.

Some teenage girls get pregnant on purpose. They think that a baby will fix problems in their lives. Some think it will solve problems with parents. Others think a baby will help a bad relationship with a boyfriend. Some teenage girls get pregnant so that they will always have someone to love and care for. Most of the time, these young women find that having a child cannot solve problems.

Having a baby means a great change. It means a responsibility that will always be yours. It means being a mother for the rest of your life.

This book is about how you can cope with becoming pregnant. Maybe you are pregnant now. This book will give you some ideas about making choices. It will help you to find advice. You should have advice before making decisions. First you must know how to make the decisions you are facing. Then you can deal with the situation.

Maybe you have a friend who is pregnant. This book will help you understand what she is going through. It will also show you the choices open for her today. Then maybe you can offer her your help.

IMPORTANT FACTS ABOUT TEEN PREGNANCY

The problem of teen pregnancy affects more and more of America's young girls every year. Did you know that:

○ More than 1 million teenage girls become pregnant every year in the United States.

○ Four out of every five pregnant teens are unmarried.

○ Every year more than 30 thousand girls under 15 years of age become pregnant.

○ Of all the girls who gave birth at the age of fifteen, 82 percent (more than four out of five) were daughters of teenage mothers.

○ Only 50 percent of the girls who have babies before they are 18 are able to complete high school.

○ It is estimated that if the trend toward teen pregnancy continues, 40 percent (four out of ten) of today's 14-year-olds will be pregnant at least once before they are 20.

○ According to a recent Harris poll, 85% of Americans consider teen pregnancy a serious national problem

Chapter 1

How Does Pregnancy Happen?

Puberty

At nine or ten years old you start to feel that you're changing. That's because you *are* changing. The changes become plainer when you're thirteen or fourteen. This strange time is called *puberty*.

At puberty your body makes new chemicals. These chemicals change the way you look. They change the way you act. The chemicals are called *hormones*. *Glands* make the chemicals and send them through the bloodstream.

Hormones do many different things. Some hormones make your bones grow longer. That makes you taller. Some hormones make your muscles become stronger. And some hormones make you grow hair where you never had hair before.

Some of the hormones make your sexual organs grow. They cause the male sex glands to make *sperm*. Sperm are germ cells carried in a liquid in a man's body. A sperm fertilizes the egg inside a woman. When a woman's egg is fertilized, she becomes pregnant.

A woman has sex glands too. They are called *ovaries*. A woman has two ovaries. They make hormones that prepare her body for a baby.

All these changes happen during puberty. Your body is growing fast. You seem to look different every day. This time can be scary and confusing. Teens in puberty often feel embarrassed. They are uncomfortable with how they look and feel.

The hormones in your body make you *look* different. They make you *think* differently. They make you *feel* different too. During puberty a teen starts to think about sexual activity.

Both male and female hormones prepare the body for *reproduction*. Reproduction means making babies.

The Reproductive System

Once you enter puberty, you can become pregnant. Some girls can become pregnant at ten or eleven years old.

But exactly how does a female become pregnant?

A woman is born with many eggs. They are in her two ovaries. During puberty the *menstrual cycle*

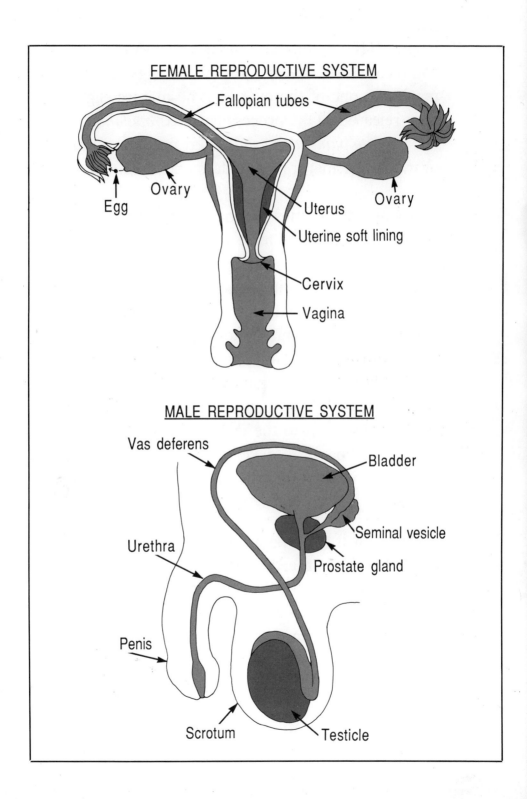

begins. This cycle takes about a month to complete. First one or more of the eggs begins to mature in one of the ovaries. The mature egg is then released. This process is called *ovulation*.

Two *fallopian tubes* are located near the woman's ovaries. The mature egg enters one of the fallopian tubes.

A woman becomes pregnant if a sperm reaches the mature egg. The male's sperm are released from his penis. The sperm travel inside the woman's vagina during sexual intercourse. Millions of sperm are released. Some sperm swim into the fallopian tubes. It only takes one of those millions of sperm to fertilize the mature egg. If a sperm fertilizes the egg, pregnancy begins.

The fertilized egg then drops into the *uterus*. The egg attaches itself to the wall of the uterus. Then the egg can begin to develop. It will be fully developed in nine months. Then a baby is ready to be born.

But what if the woman has not become pregnant? The unfertilized egg still travels to the uterus. But now it will be pushed out along with other material. This is the process of *menstruation*. It happens every month if the woman has not become pregnant.

Chapter 2

Making The Best Decision

I t is very hard to make decisions about an un-planned pregnancy. It is even hard for an adult married couple with children. Imagine how hard it is for a teenage girl still in school!

Facts and Feelings

There are many ways to make an important decision. The most important part of decision-making is *GETTING ALL THE FACTS*. Nobody can make a good decision without facts.

Another very important part of decision-making is *KNOWING YOUR FEELINGS*. All decisions involve *feelings*. You need to know your feelings. It is the best way to make good decisions.

People can become scared and upset. Sometimes they feel depressed. These are hard times for making decisions.

Judy reaches out for help by writing to her guidance counselor.

Ms. Margaret Cummings, Student Counselor
The Hill School

Dear Ms. Cummings,
   I have a problem. I have thought about it for two weeks. I don't know what to do. I am very confused. I am also very scared.
   I think I may be pregnant. But I don't know. I don't know what it feels like. I'm not sure.
   I cannot tell my parents. They won't understand. They'll get mad. And I'm too embarrassed.
   Can I come and talk to you this week? I wrote this note because I was too ashamed to talk to you in person.

                                                    Signed,

                                                    Judy Meadows

Seeking help from a guidance counselor is one way to make decision-making easier. Guidance counselors listen to problems carefully. They can often help to sort out your thoughts and feelings.

There is another way to make decision-making easier. To begin, write down lists of "facts and

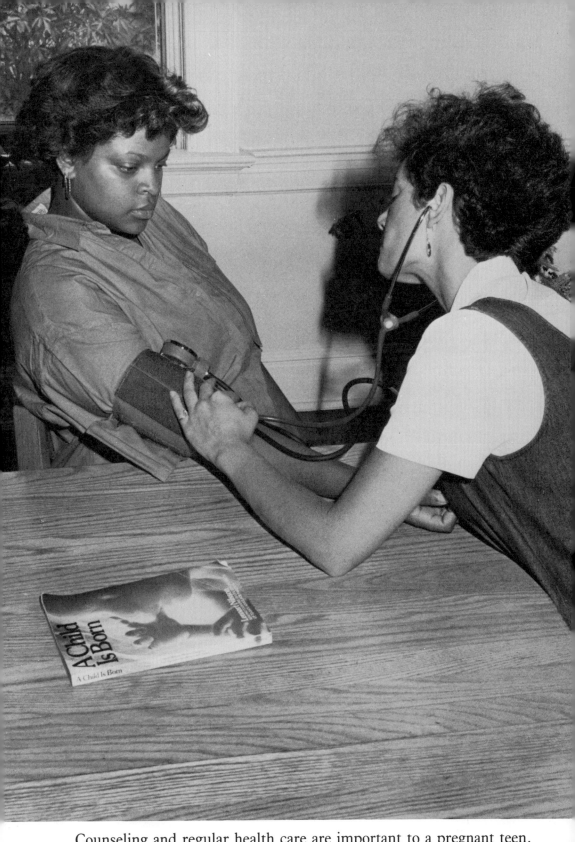
Counseling and regular health care are important to a pregnant teen.

feelings." Make sure to list every choice you can think of. Take time to think carefully about each possible choice. Then make a list of "pros" (for) and "cons" (against). Divide a piece of paper into two sides. Put "pros" (good points) on one side. Put "cons" (bad points) on the other side. Then think about each point. Are there more pros or cons? This can help you see whether you have enough information to make a good decision.

Deciding What To Do First

The first step is putting facts and feelings down on paper. Then it is time to figure out which ones are most important. The most important ones go to the top of the list. This is called *setting priorities.* Priorities put things in order. They help you to remember which things are most important. Having priorities makes decision-making easier. A friendly "listener" can help to set priorities. A letter to an old friend, Sunday school teacher, or scout leader is another way to define the problem so that a solution is in sight. Valerie chose to write to Cindy, a pen pal for many years.

Dear Cindy,
   Things are not going too well. Since I wrote to you things have changed. I got pregnant. It was a total accident. I don't really know what to do. I know Chris is the father. But he doesn't want to help me. I don't

know what my parents will say. They might kick me out. I don't know. I'll have to find somewhere to live. Maybe I'll get a job. I might like working as a receptionist. I'll have to drop out of school. I have no idea. I'll just deal with it as it comes.

I don't have anyone here to talk to. You're the only one. Call me sometime? You know my number.

Love,
Valerie

Dear Valerie,

Your letter sounded like you need someone to talk to besides me. You have a lot of decisions to make.

If you really can't talk to your parents, please try to talk to a school counselor or your minister. Have you seen a doctor? A doctor will tell you if you are healthy and will have a normal pregnancy.

You can't just "deal with it as it comes." You must decide what you can handle, especially since you say you are alone. Having the baby and caring for yourself will be very difficult. And it will be hard to find work if you haven't finished school.

Motherhood lasts a lifetime. Someone with experience will be able to help you decide what to do.

Please write to me again. I care about you. I want to know who you talked things over with, and what you have decided. I want to be sure you are taking care of yourself.

Love from your friend,
Cindy

Talking things over with parents can help.

Things to Consider

A pregnant teenager has many questions. You must ask your questions as you think about your future. Here are some important things to think about:

○ **Age and maturity.** Sometimes there are health risks for a girl who is pregnant at a young age. These risks may affect the mother or the baby. Sometimes there are risks for both the mother *and* the baby. A doctor should always be asked about these risks.

You must also think about your own maturity. How old do you feel and act? Do you feel ready to take the responsibilities of pregnancy? Or a newborn baby? Or a child as it grows up? These are questions for careful thought. Often you think of yourself as a grown-up when you are not. It may help to get an honest opinion from someone else.

○ **The father.** You must think about the father. He is the other person who is most affected by the situation. You know who the father is. You must find out if he will help. Will he help you with money? Will he help you with emotional support? Will he be a good father? Is he mature and responsible? Can you raise a baby without him?

Sometimes you do not know for sure who the father is. Sometimes he has gone away. Sometimes he is just "out of the picture." Then other questions must be faced. Are you willing for your baby to grow up without a father? Can you make it on your own?

○ **Home.** A baby must have a home. Maybe it can be with your family. Or maybe it can be with the father's family. Maybe you can live on your own. Maybe you and your child can live with friends. You must figure out how the home will function. If you live with others, who will be in charge? Whose rules will the baby follow? Can the new home support a baby?

○ **Money.** A pregnant teen must also think about money. Having a baby is expensive. Medical costs are very high. You must pay for food and clothing (for both yourself and the child). Other costly items are needed, such as baby bottles, diapers, and a crib. Are you old enough to get a

job? Would you be able to keep the job when
the baby is born? Even if you can get a job, it
may not pay enough to support yourself and the
baby. And you might need to pay a baby-sitter
or day care center. Money is one thing that you
will always need. A young girl may get some
help from public sources. It is important for you
to find out as soon as possible if you qualify for
help.

○ **Your family.** Support from your family is very
   important. You must think about whether your
   family can give you any help. This help may be
   money. It may be a place to live. Or it may be
   emotional comfort. If you are lucky it is all
   three. A young mother and child need a safe,
   loving place to live. With security they will have
   a much easier time.
   It is possible that no support will come from
your family. Then you must decide if you can
have a child on your own.

○ **Health history.** You must think about your
   health. You must know if you have any health
   problems. Some problems might make
   pregnancy dangerous or difficult. You must also
   know if there are health problems that would
   affect the baby. A mother or a father may carry
   a disease. Such a disease can be harmful to a
   fetus (developing baby).

If you become pregnant, there are many new responsibilities to consider.

Some diseases are passed through families.
Family diseases are called *hereditary* diseases. If a
pregnant girl carries a hereditary disease, there is a
chance that her baby will be born with it.

Some diseases are picked up by a mother or
father in later years. They can affect an unborn
child too. People get them from having sex with a
person who has the disease. Venereal diseases (VD)
are the most common. These include syphilis,
gonorrhea, genital herpes, and acquired immune
deficiency syndrome (AIDS).

Taking drugs can also hurt your unborn child.
Many prescription drugs can be harmful. There are
also illegal drugs, such as marijuana, cocaine and
crack, "uppers," "downers," LSD, and heroin.
These, as well as cigarettes and alcohol, are very
harmful to a fetus.

There may be some danger even if you took
drugs *before* your pregnancy. There may be damage
if you had certain x-rays. That is why every
pregnant woman should see a doctor. You should
tell your doctor your medical history. The doctor
will then decide if anything in the history could
have a bad effect on the fetus.

○ **When the baby is due.** For some teens an
   abortion is a possible choice. In an abortion a
   doctor ends a pregnancy. You must know certain
   things if you are thinking about abortion. You
   must know how long you have been pregnant.

The pregnancy may be too far along. Then an abortion may not be possible. We will talk more about abortion in Chapter 6.

○ **The future.** A baby changes its mother's life very much. A pregnant teen must think about the future. What are the things you may not be able to do once a child is born? Do you want to finish high school? Go to college? Have a professional career? Can you do those things with a baby?

○ **Personal beliefs.** You must also think about things that are not just practical. Personal beliefs are very important. They are part of making decisions too. Your religious views may limit your choices. For some people, abortion will not be possible. Others don't want to raise a child in a one-parent family. It all depends on personal feelings.

○ **Mental outlook.** You must step back and look at yourself. That is hard to do. You must figure out *why* you are making certain decisions. Teenagers often make decisions out of fear. Other times, they try to do what others want. It is important for you to make decisions slowly and carefully.

Those are the things that you should think about. Any woman who wants to have a baby should think about them carefully. Some of them are special problems of teens who become pregnant by accident. All of them are very serious.

Pregnancy is a time of many changes. Read and get as much information as possible.

Chapter 3

What Being Pregnant is Like

A normal pregnancy lasts forty weeks, about nine months. *Trimesters* divide the pregnancy into three parts. The first trimester is the first three months. The second trimester is the second three months. The third trimester is the last three months. How does a teenager feel during pregnancy? It is important for you to understand these changes inside you.

Sally and Trish have been friends since the fourth grade. Now that Trish is pregnant, she needs her friend more than ever.

First Trimester

Sally Wethers
187 Fort Drake Rd.
Drumville, MN 09552

Dear Sally,
   Well, it's been two months. And I feel lousy! I can
hardly stay awake sometimes. And I get over 14 hours
of sleep a day! I still wake up in the morning and feel
like barfing.
   The other stuff isn't so great either. I feel achy, and
sore. And every time I smell sardines, I feel like throwing up.
   David was talking about the car the other day. And
right in the middle of it I burst into tears. David thinks
I'm going nuts. I don't know. The doctor said I would
be very emotional.
   More later. I'm falling asleep at my desk.

                                                    Love,

                                                    Trish

   During the first three months a pregnant woman
may feel ill. It is common to feel nausea or
"morning sickness." Nausea is feeling sick to your
stomach. Certain tastes or smells (such as cigarette
smoke or perfume) can be a problem. They can
make pregnant women feel like throwing up. Some
women only feel sick at a certain time of day.

Others feel "morning sickness" all day long. Breasts often become larger. They often feel sore. Many women feel very tired during the first trimester. Some pregnant teens try to keep up with school during this time. They may feel especially tired.

Three months have gone by. The embryo is now called a fetus. The sex of the fetus can be seen. The fetus is about three inches long.

Second Trimester

Sally Wethers
187 Fort Drake Rd.
Drumville, MN 09552

Dear Sally,

I'm feeling so much better! It's great! I'm almost five months pregnant and I feel great! My morning sickness went away. And I don't feel so tired. I may actually make it!

And guess what? I felt the baby move! For the first time. I couldn't believe it! I felt awfully weird!

Just thought I'd keep you posted. See you next Saturday.

Love,

Trish

Many women find the second trimester to be the easiest. Usually the morning sickness has gone away. The tiredness is not so bad. It is now that the belly starts to get big (if it hasn't already). And you can feel the fetus move.

Six months have gone by. The fetus now looks more like a baby. It is usually eleven to fourteen inches long.

Third Trimester

Sally Wethers
187 Fort Drake Rd.
Drumville, MN 09552

Dear Sally,

I'm getting SO nervous! Sally, I can't tell you. It's only three weeks away! What if something happens? What if David can't get me to the hospital?

My ankles look like golf balls. And my back is killing me. Try carrying around ten pounds every day for a couple of months. It tires you out! And I'm so fat! I haven't seen my own feet in four weeks! David says he likes me fat. I hate it.

I can't wait. I just can't wait for this to be over. I'm ready. I'm really ready. Pretty soon, I'll have a baby. I don't believe it.

I have to stop now. I'm crying all over your letter.

I'll keep you posted.

Love,

Trish

By the third trimester most women are eager for it to be over. The last three months are very tiring. It is difficult to sleep. Simple actions like bending over are hard to do. Even getting out of a chair is not easy. Often women are both excited and nervous at this time. They wonder what birth will be like. They wonder if it will hurt. They wonder if the baby will be healthy.

Nine months have gone by. By the end of the third trimester the baby is ready to be born. It is fully developed. It can weigh from six to ten pounds.

A Time of Changes

Those are the many changes a pregnant woman's body goes through. And they all happen within nine months. If the pregnant woman is a teenager, she must also deal with puberty. And puberty causes many changes, too.

Many changes that happen during pregnancy are not physical. Many changes are emotional. Hormones cause the physical changes. But they also cause changes in your mood. If you are usually a calm person, you may get moody when you are pregnant. That is because of hormonal changes. Pregnancy causes many other changes in your life. You may have to find new ways to deal with your friends. You will treat your parents differently. And being in school will be different.

Right from the start of a pregnancy, a healthy diet is important.

Chapter 4

Caring For Yourself and Your Baby

Guidance counselors, doctors, friends, and family all want to help you have a healthy pregnancy and a well baby if you choose to become a teen mother. Dr. Stone is Franny's physician. Her job is to guide Franny during her pregnancy so that both mother and baby stay well.

If you are pregnant your most important job is taking care of yourself. That is especially true for a teenager. A teenager's own body is still growing and developing.

From the desk of
Donna S. Stone, M.D.

Dear Franny,

I'm glad you came in to see me last week. I wanted to talk to you about your visit. I wanted to remind you about a few things.

First, your diet. Remember to eat plenty of dairy products and plenty of good proteins—eggs, and meat, and fish. That doesn't mean a chicken sandwich at the fast-food place. That means real food. Homemade.

If you want to snack, don't go for corn chips or chocolate bars. Have an apple or a banana. And drink plenty of fluids, especially water.

Remember to do the exercises I gave you.

Any questions, just call me. I want to make sure you have a happy, healthy baby, and I want to make sure *you* stay healthy as well!

Best regards,

Dr. Stone

Eating Right

All teenagers need lots of good food. They need foods full of protein. They need vitamins and minerals to help them grow. They also need food to give them energy. They need energy for their active lives. As a pregnant woman you also need lots of good food. You need strength for pregnancy. And you must give nutrients to a growing fetus.

Pregnancy is not the time to go on a diet. But it is also not an excuse to eat fattening junk foods. You need foods that are high in vitamins but low in calories. You are *not* eating for two.   *90-17279*

FOODS THAT ARE GOOD FOR YOU

Dairy products

These provide calcium, protein, and vitamins. They are important for building strong bones and teeth. They help a fetus develop strong bones and teeth too. Foods in this group are lowfat milk, cheese, yogurt, and ice cream.

Meat, fish, eggs and nuts

These provide protein, iron and vitamins. These give nutrients to the brain and the blood. They help keep you and your fetus strong. Foods in this group are beef, chicken, seafood, eggs, beans, and peanut butter.

Grains

These provide iron, vitamins, and carbohydrates. Carbohydrates supply "fuel" for the body. The body "burns" the fuel and turns it into energy. Grains also help the nervous system and blood to grow. Foods in this group are whole wheat bread, rice, pasta, cereal, tortillas, pancakes, muffins, and grits.

Fruits and vegetables

These provide many vitamins and minerals. They help teeth and bones to grow. They help the body fight infections. It is best to eat a variety of fruits and vegetables every day. Dark green vegetables such as spinach and greens are especially good.

Lourdes High School Library
4034 West 56th Street
Chicago. Illinois 60629

Lots of water

Water helps to digest food. It helps your body use the nutrients. It also helps to get rid of bodily waste.

FOODS TO STAY AWAY FROM

○ **Salt** Salt can be a problem, especially when you are pregnant. Salt makes the body hold water. Pregnant women often have swollen ankles. Other parts of the body can swell, too. This is because the body is holding too much water. Swelling is uncomfortable. Cutting down on salt can ease this problem. Too much salt can also lead to high blood pressure.

○ **Sweet and greasy foods** Pastries, cakes, and cookies are high in sugar and fats. They are low in nutrients.

○ **Caffeine and other drugs** It is important to stay away from caffeine during pregnancy. Caffeine is a drug. It can cause problems for a developing fetus. It speeds up the heart. It affects the blood system. Foods that contain caffeine are coffee, tea, dark sodas (colas and root beer) and chocolate. Some buffered aspirin also contains caffeine.

○ **Alcohol** Alcohol is dangerous during pregnancy. If you drink alcohol during pregnancy it can harm your baby. The baby may be born with mental problems. Or physical problems.

○ **Smoking.** Smoking during pregnancy causes problems too. Smoking can harm both you and the fetus. Smoking makes veins and arteries (blood vessels) become smaller. That means the heart has to work harder to get enough blood to the rest of the body. Babies whose mothers smoke usually weigh less. They are not as strong at birth as other babies. Smoking also makes your breathing harder.

○ **Drugs.** Other drugs are harmful too. Marijuana and cocaine. Heroin. Amphetamines (uppers) and barbiturates (downers). These are all very dangerous to a fetus. You should remember that addiction is passed on. If you are addicted to something, your fetus will be born addicted. You should stay away from *all* drugs. Even "over-the-counter" drugs such as aspirin and cold capsules. Diet pills, nose drops, douches, laxatives, and acne cream can also cause problems. You should *always* ask a doctor before using any kind of medication.

Whatever you eat, the fetus eats. Whatever you drink or smoke, the fetus does too. Remembering this can make it easier to stick to healthful foods during pregnancy.

Exercise is Good

Most teens can continue to exercise throughout pregnancy. Most light exercises are safe. Walking and swimming are good. They are safe for just about everyone. Exercise relieves stress. It makes mothers more comfortable. It makes them more relaxed during pregnancy. Exercise strengthens muscles. It also increases endurance. And that makes giving birth easier. Strong, healthy mothers recover quickly from giving birth. They are also better prepared to take care of a new baby.

Special Exercises for Pregnant Women

There are special types of exercises for pregnant women. These exercises strengthen the lower back. They also strengthen the stomach and leg muscles. Those muscles take the most strain during pregnancy and childbirth. Good posture makes pregnancy easier. Safe ways to bend and lift also help. Good posture also cuts down on back strain.

Special exercise classes are given for pregnant women and teens. One of the most popular exercise programs is Lamaze (pronounced la-mahz). Lamaze classes are for a mother-to-be and a partner. The partner may be the baby's father. Or it may be a friend or relative. Lamaze classes teach special breathing exercises that make childbirth easier.

You will want to get back in shape after your baby is born. Join an exercise class for mothers and babies. It will be fun for both of you.

Don't Forget the Importance of Sleep

A big part of being fit is getting plenty of rest. A pregnant teen may be especially tired during the first trimester. You may need to take daytime naps. It can be hard to find time for school and friends.

HOW AN EGG IS FERTILIZED

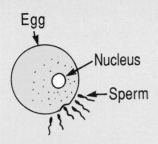

Egg
Nucleus
Sperm

Sperm cell enters egg.

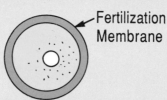
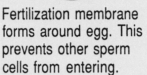

Fertilization Membrane

Fertilization membrane forms around egg. This prevents other sperm cells from entering.

Sperm nucleus and egg nucleus combine. Egg is now ready to start dividing.

DEVELOPMENT OF THE FETUS

First Trimester

1st month   2nd month   3rd month

Second Trimester

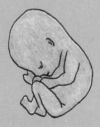

4th month   5th month   6th month

Third Trimester

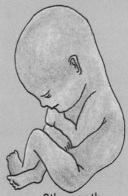

7th month   8th month   9th month

Some teenagers need to work. Others need to set up a new home. Eating right will give you the energy needed for these tasks. Exercise and sleep help you to cope better with your life.

Pre-Natal Care (Care Before Giving Birth)

If you decide to continue your pregnancy and raise your child, you have a lot to do. First you should see a doctor. The doctor will give you a complete examination. You can also get information on pregnancy care. A doctor who takes care of pregnant women is called an *obstetrician*. An obstetrician also delivers babies. Midwives also deliver babies. There are many ways to find an obstetrician or a midwife. Most family doctors can recommend an obstetrician. Hospitals have obstetricians or midwives they can recommend.

You should have regular check-ups throughout your pregnancy. The doctor will want to know all about you. The doctor will need to know when your last normal period began. This will help to figure out when you became pregnant. Then the doctor will know when the baby is due. The doctor will also do an examination. The exam will show the size of the uterus. This helps to tell how far along the pregnancy is.

The doctor may use a test called a *sonogram*. A sonogram uses sound waves to get a picture of the fetus. Sometimes doctors use sonograms later in pregnancy. It helps them look for problems as the fetus grows.

Tell the doctor about any drugs or medications that you have taken. Especially any drugs you have taken since you became pregnant. Ask the doctor before you take any medication, even aspirin. You may decide to breastfeed your baby. Then you will need to be careful about medicines even after the baby is born. Medicines will be passed to the baby in your milk.

You should also avoid x-rays during pregnancy. X-rays can upset the normal growth of a fetus.

Special Risks

As a teen you have special risks during pregnancy. You are more likely to give birth to a *premature* baby. Premature babies are born earlier than the full nine months. These babies are more likely to have birth defects. They also have a greater chance of getting infections after birth. You run the risk of getting *toxemia* and *anemia*. Toxemia makes the hands and feet swell. It also causes high blood pressure. Anemia makes you tired and weak. The doctor should take blood tests and urine tests. Your blood pressure should be checked often.

A healthy mother means a healthy baby.

Certain basic things are needed for a new baby.

Preparing for the New Baby

Once you decide to raise your child, you must
plan for a new life with your baby. A baby needs a
cradle or crib to sleep in. A baby also needs clothes
and diapers, blankets, powders, soaps, and creams.
You must decide between breastfeeding or
bottlefeeding. You may need bottles and formula
(milk-like food for a new baby). These basics must
be ready when you and your baby come home
from the hospital.

Arriving Home

You need other things, too, when you get home from the hospital. You need support. Many mothers feel very sad and lonely after giving birth, even those who keep their babies. This feeling is called post-partum depression. The baby's father may help care for the baby. Or maybe friends and relatives will help. This kind of help makes a new mother feel better. A group of other teenage mothers may also be a great help. They can be a comfort. Talking to people like yourself is good.

Family and friends can help a young mother care for her baby.

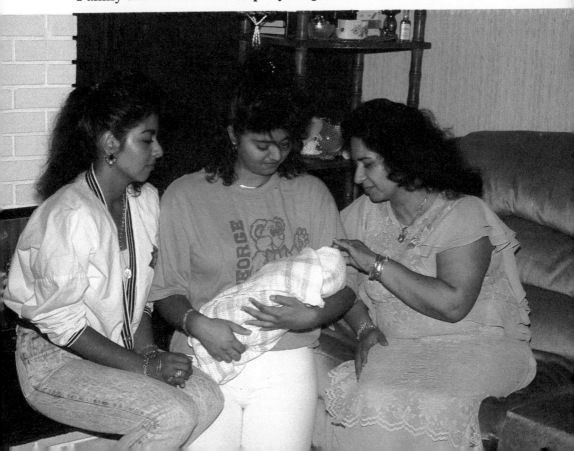

It can help you feel less alone. It is also a good way to share information on child care.

A baby needs medical care after it is born. Before it was born an obstetrician cared for mother and baby. A doctor who takes care of babies is called a *pediatrician*. A doctor who delivered the baby can probably recommend a pediatrician. A newborn infant needs regular checkups. Sometimes a newborn needs to see a pediatrician every few weeks.

You must get out of the house once in a while. It is good to get away from your baby sometimes. Some mothers cannot find people to babysit even once in a while. They can feel trapped and upset. They may take their anger out by screaming at the baby. They may become so upset that they hit the baby. That is often how child abuse begins. That is why support is so important for teenage mothers.

A Lifetime Decision

Choosing to raise a child is very difficult. It is a choice that lasts a long time. You will be a caregiver for eighteen years or more. Help and support from others makes things a lot easier. Keeping a baby may be the best decision for some teens. If you are mature, you may be ready for the responsibilities of motherhood.

Chapter 5

Choosing Adoption

We have already talked about the things you should do if you want to have a baby. We talked about what it is like to be pregnant for nine months. We have also talked about raising a baby.

But carrying a fetus for nine months is not right for everyone. Neither is giving birth. Neither is being a mother to a newborn baby. You may decide against motherhood. Abortion and adoption are two other choices you may think about.

In this chapter we will talk about adoption.

What Is Adoption?

Adoption is easy to understand. A woman gives birth to a baby. Then she turns it over to an adoption agency. The mother gives up all her legal rights to the child. The adoption agency finds a home for the baby. The agency often finds a married couple who cannot have children of their own. For them, adopting a baby brings great joy. Carol is unsure about her ability to raise a child on her own. She remembers Janis Stein, a girl she met while at work three years ago. Janis decided to give her baby up for adoption. In writing to Janis, Carol is hoping to understand more about adoption.

Dear Janis,

It's been a long time. I haven't heard from you. I hope everything is alright.

Things are alright with me. Actually, I'm pregnant. And I'm trying to think about what to do.

I'm writing to you because you know about adoption. I know that you put your baby up for adoption three years ago. I know it must have been hard. What did you do?

People tell me that I would never see the baby. Not if I put it up for adoption. Is that true? I don't know if I can live with that.

Does it cost money? How do you go about doing it? When do I have to decide? I can't keep my baby. I'm not ready. I couldn't be a mom. But I don't want an abortion either. Can you live knowing your baby is somewhere out there? And you don't know where?

I'd really appreciate some advice.

Best regards,
Carol

Some married couples who can't have children of their own are
happy to adopt babies.

Some things about adoption can be hard for you
to accept. One thing is the hardest. *You will never
be allowed to see your baby after it is born.* You will
not even know who adopted your baby. Adoption
agencies will not tell. That may seem mean, but it
is necessary. Adoption must be a decision that a
mother cannot change.

Thinking About Adoption

You may be thinking about adoption. You
should talk to an adoption agency. It is best to talk
to more than one agency. Each agency has its own
rules and its own way of doing things.

A good agency will have a counselor for you to
talk to. The counselor discusses adoption with you.
A counselor should help you think about your
choices. You should talk about your reasons for
adoption. You should also be told your rights and
your responsibilities.

An agency should *never* make you feel that you
must go through the adoption. You must have
plenty of time to think. It is a very hard decision to
make. No one should ever try to rush it.

It is very difficult to decide to give up a baby.
You may change your mind many times during
pregnancy. That's okay. You can change your
mind as many times as you want until the legal
papers are signed. A good agency waits until the
baby is born. Then they ask the mother to sign the
papers.

Agencies are usually very careful about finding adoptive parents. Interested couples must show the agency that they will be good parents. It is like applying for a difficult job. The couple are asked many questions.

People from the agency then visit the couple's home to see how they live. An adoption agency want to know how much money the couple make. It also asks for letters from people who know the couple. In the letters, friends or coworkers can say if they think the couple would be good parents.

Remember that you will probably never know who the adoptive parents are. And the adopting parents will never know who you are. This is the policy of most agencies.

When the adoption agreement is signed, the baby is given a new birth certificate. It is then the duty of the adoptive parents to name the child.

After the Adoptive Parents Take the Baby Home

The adoptive parents take the baby home. Then there may be a waiting period. It may be six months to a year. Until then the adoption is not final. A worker from the agency visits the child's new home during this time. The worker will see how the baby and the parents are doing. The worker makes sure that the baby is treated properly.

A social worker visits the adopting parents. She checks to see that the baby is being cared for properly.

The adoption is final after the waiting period. The legal papers are then sealed. The mother can never get the child back.

Private Adoptions

It may be possible to have a private adoption. Someone outside the family will take the child. This might be done with help from a family doctor. Or someone in the community, such as a priest or a rabbi, may arrange it. A lawyer would be called. The lawyer will probably draw up an agreement. The adoptive couple usually pay some expenses for the pregnant teen. The expenses may include medical costs. They may also cover living expenses and lawyer's fees.

Private adoptions are different from agency adoptions. They are often not as strict. Adopting couples may be friends of the family. Or they may be friends of friends. They are not as carefully chosen. They do not go through the tests that an agency insists on.

Things to Think About

Many people cannot have children of their own. Many of these people have good jobs and fine homes. Many people want healthy infants for adoption.

Some people may offer a pregnant woman a lot
of money for her child. They may pressure her.
Before the baby is born they may ask her to agree
to give it up. They may offer so much money that
the mother has a hard time saying no. Many
mothers give up their unborn baby for money. But
many who do are sorry later. They regret their
decisions.

A woman must think hard if she is offered
money for her child. She must be careful. It is easy
to make a choice that she will regret.

Choosing the Right Agency

Can your agency be trusted? It is very important
to find out. There are ways to check on an agency.
Here are some things to remember:

1.   Seek Good Advice. Some of the names and
     phone numbers on page 61 will be helpful.
     These organizations can tell you which
     agencies are the best.
2.   Ask for Papers and Proof of Certification. You
     should always ask to see the agency's papers.
     These should include certificates and licenses.
     They show that the agency is allowed to
     operate in a given state. An agency should also
     be registered or connected with a larger group.
3.   Ask How Long the Agency Has Been
     Running. If the agency has been around for a
     long time, it is probably trustworthy.

Other Things to Think About

It is best to put a baby up for adoption right away. An infant has the best chance of finding a good home. Most adoptive couples want a newborn baby.

This is the hardest time for you to give your baby away, though. A newborn baby is cute and cuddly.

It is important to think about the child. An older child will not be adopted very easily. It may never be adopted. Most people do not want to adopt a child over the age of one year. Children who are not adopted before their first birthday often spend the rest of their childhood in foster homes. Some are put into state-run orphanages. These children often grow up to be very unhappy people.

A Tough Decision, But Often a Good One

Putting a baby up for adoption is always a very hard decision. But for many pregnant teens it is often the best thing to do.

Many teenagers know they are too young for the responsibilities of parenthood. Many teens feel too unsure of themselves to be good parents. Many teens do not want to end their pregnancies with an abortion. For them, adoption may be the best solution.

Chapter 6

Choosing Abortion

"**H**ello. Is this Rose Trellin? This is Dr. Kathy Simmons, from the Sandon Clinic. The receptionist said you had some questions, and left your number.

"No, abortions are not dangerous. Especially early ones. They are simple enough to be done right here at the clinic. You can come in and leave the same day.

"That's right. Only abortions of very advanced pregnancies need to be done in hospitals.

"There are lots of different methods. It depends on how far along the pregnancy has gone. We can talk later about the different methods.

"You can come in and talk to a counselor any time you like. There are always people here for you to talk to. They can answer all your questions. Or you can call me again.

"Please come in and see me when you visit the clinic. Goodbye."

Many pregnant teens do not feel ready to have a baby. Some feel they can't raise a child. Others feel they can't put their child up for adoption. These teens often choose to end a pregnancy before the fetus can live outside the uterus. That is called *abortion*. In this chapter we will discuss the different types of abortions.

Menstrual Extraction

One type of abortion is *menstrual extraction*. This is done early in the pregnancy. "Menstrual" has to do with blood and tissue in the uterus. "Extraction" means "to take out." This kind of abortion is usually done before the sixth week of pregnancy. Sometimes it is done even before a pregnancy test can tell for sure. With this method, a thin tube is used. It is put into the *cervix,* or opening of the uterus. The tube is attached to a suction machine. The suction machine removes the contents of the uterus.

Menstrual extraction is not expensive. It is more or less painless. It can be done in a doctor's office, or in a clinic. It has some drawbacks, however. First, this method is not common. It may be hard to find a doctor who does menstrual extractions. Second, it can only be done very early in the pregnancy. Third, many teens have irregular periods. They cannot be sure they are pregnant. Some teens rush to get a menstrual extraction even though they aren't pregnant.

Suction (Vacuum Aspiration)

The most common abortion is done with *suction* or *vacuum aspiration*. "Aspiration" means "to suck something out" or to remove it. This method is usually used during six to twelve weeks of pregnancy. It may be performed as late as the twenty-fourth week. It has two or three steps.

○ First, the doctor *dilates*, or opens, the cervix. This may be done with thin metal rods. They push the cervix open bit by bit.

○ A thin suction tube is used after the cervix is dilated. It is put into the cervix. This part of the procedure is similar to menstrual extraction, but the tube is a bit larger. Suction is used to remove the fetus. The lining of the uterus is also removed.

○ Some doctors add a third step. They want to be sure that the uterus is empty. They use a thin metal instrument called a *curette*. They gently scrape the sides of the uterus. This makes sure that it is free of tissue. This step is called *curettage*.

About Anesthesia

Suction abortions are usually done in a clinic or a hospital. They rarely need an overnight stay. A patient can often choose whether to stay awake or be asleep. She will probably be given a choice between two kinds of *anesthesia*. Anesthesia makes the body numb. When the body is numb it does not feel anything. Anesthesia is used to make abortions more comfortable.

A patient may want to stay awake. She will probably be given *local* anesthesia. This will make her cervix numb. The patient may choose to go to sleep. She will get *general* anesthesia.

Saline Abortion (or Induction)

A third type of abortion is done after sixteen weeks of pregnancy. This type is almost always done in a hospital. It is called a *saline* abortion. Saline means "salt water."

The doctor uses a hollow needle to remove some fluid from the pregnancy sac. The doctor then injects salt water into the pregnancy sac. The salt water causes early labor. The fetus is pushed out of the body, usually within three days. A fetus cannot survive outside the uterus this early. The salt solution usually causes the fetus to stop functioning even before it is delivered.

The Right Place to Have an Abortion

How can you find a safe place to have an abortion? You can ask your doctor. That is the best place to start. Your doctor may not be able to do

the abortion. Or the doctor's fee might be too
expensive. The doctor will usually recommend
another doctor or a good clinic. Planned Parenthood
is a helpful organization. It has branches all over
the country.

Questions of Safety

Early abortion is quite safe. It is one of the safest
kinds of surgery. Very few patients have problems
from early abortions. Most problems that do arise
are minor. The longer the pregnancy, the greater
the chance of problems. But any abortion should
be safe if it is done correctly. Even a late abortion
is less risky than delivering a baby at nine months.

Many people worry about abortions. They think
an abortion will make it difficult to have children
later. It won't.

Legal Rights

In the United States, abortion has been legal
since 1973. First trimester abortions (up to three
months) are legal in every state. Second trimester
abortions (up to six months) may be controlled by
each state. Still, the final decision is the patient's
and the doctor's. Some states can forbid third
trimester abortions (six to nine months), except
when the mother's life is in danger.

Chapter 7

About Birth Control

Condoms are the most common
birth control method. They are
also a protection against AIDS.

You have read about being pregnant as a teenager. You can see it is not easy. It is a serious and
difficult situation. But there are ways to prevent it.
These ways are called birth control. Birth control
devices prevent pregnancy.

There are many methods of birth control. They
are for men and women. Some methods are more
effective than others. *None will work 100 percent of
the time.*

Of course, there is one 100 percent reliable
method of birth control. It is *abstinence, the*
decision *not to have sexual intercourse.* Many teens
think this is the best choice of all.

Some people are against birth control. Some
religions forbid using birth control. But it is a
choice each person must make. The following are
the most popular birth control products:

○ **Condom**

A condom is a thin rubber case.
The male rolls the condom up over
his erect penis. The case holds the
sperm. It prevents sperm from
swimming into the vagina during
sex. Condoms can be bought in
drug stores without a prescription.
They should only be used once.

○ **Diaphragm and
contraceptive jelly or cream**

One of the most popular birth
control methods for women is the
diaphragm (di-a-fram). A woman
must be fitted for a diaphragm by a
doctor. A diaphragm is a rubber
cap that fits in the vagina over the
opening of the uterus (cervix). The
cap stops sperm from swimming
into the uterus during sex. The cap
also holds contraceptive jelly or
cream. Either of these can be used
to kill sperm.

○ **The Pill**

A popular birth control method for
women is "the pill." It may be the
most effective. But the pill is not
right for everyone. It may be
harmful to some women's health.
And it may cause side effects (bad
reactions in the body). A doctor
should *always* be asked about its
use. *The pill must be used as
directed.*

○ **IUD's**

IUD's, or "intra uterine devices,"
are another form of birth control
for women. An IUD is placed in
the uterus by a doctor. It may be
left in for over a year. Many
people question whether they are
completely safe. It is recommended
mostly for adult women. A doctor
should *always* be asked about the
use of IUD's.

○ **Spermicidal jellies,
cream, and foams**

You can get spermicidal jellies,
creams, and foams in any
drugstore. A prescription is not
necessary. These preparations kill
sperm on contact. Each must be
used by a woman *before* sex.
Foams, creams, and jellies must be
applied into the vagina. They kill
sperm that may enter during sex.

○ **Contraceptive Sponge**

A recently developed contraceptive
that is 90% effective when used
correctly is the contraceptive
sponge. It is inexpensive and easy
to use. It acts as a barrier at the
cervix, like a diaphragm, but does
not have to be fitted by a doctor.
The sponge itself absorbs the
sperm, preventing it from traveling
toward the uterus. And it is
pretreated with spermicide. It must
be used according to the directions
for it to be completely safe.

Glossary—*Explaining New Words*

abortion   The process of ending a pregnancy.

Acquired Immune Deficiency Syndrome (AIDS)
A sexually transmitted disease (STD) that attacks
the body's immune system.

adoption   Process of giving a baby to parents
other than the natural parents.

amniotic fluid   Fluid in the pregnancy sac.

amniotic sac   The pregnancy sac.

anemia   Condition that makes a person feel weak
and tired all the time.

anesthesia   Gas or other chemical used to make
the body feel numb.

cervix   Opening of the uterus.

contraception   Prevention of pregnancy.

curette   Thin metal instrument used to open the
cervix.

curettage   Process of cleaning the walls of the
uterus with a curette.

dilate   To open.

embryo   Term for a pregnancy during the first
two months.

fallopian tubes   Tubes near the ovaries where the
egg is fertilized.

fertilization   The beginning of reproduction.

fetus   Term for pregnancy after three months.

hereditary   Passed down through the blood of a
family.

hormones   Chemicals in the body that stimulate
growth or change.

59

menstruation   Monthly loss of blood and other materials from the uterus.

obstetrician   Doctor who specializes in childbirth.

ovaries   Female sex glands that hold a female's eggs.

ovulation   The releasing of a mature egg.

ovum   A mature egg.

pediatrician   Doctor who specializes in the care of children.

placenta   Vitamin-rich lining of the uterus during pregnancy.

premature   Not fully developed.

prenatal   Before birth.

puberty   Time of growth, change, and sexual maturity early in the teenage years.

sonogram   Picture of pregnancy made by a machine using sound waves.

sperm   Male fertilizing fluid.

syphilis   A sexually transmitted disease.

testes   Male sex glands.

testosterone   Male hormone that makes sex organs grow.

umbilical cord   Cord that carries food and oxygen to a fetus from the placenta.

uterus   Organ in which a fetus develops. It is also called a womb.

vacuum aspiration   The process of taking out or removing by the use of suction.

venereal disease (VD)   Sexually transmitted disease.

Where To Go For Help

Planned Parenthood Federation of America
810 Seventh Avenue
New York, NY 10019
Telephone: (212) 541-7800

National Committee for Adoption
2052 M Street NW, Suite 512
Washington, DC 20036
Telephone: (202) 463-7559

Birthright
686 North Broad St.
Woodbury, NJ 08096
Telephone: (609) 848-1819

Alternatives to Abortion International
46 North Broadway
Yonkers, NY 10701
Telephone: (914) 423-6666

National Adoption Exchange
1218 Chestnut Street
Philadelphia, PA 19107
Telephone: (215) 925-0200

National Association of Parents and Professionals for
   Safe Alternatives in Childbirth
P.O. Box 428
Marble Hill, MO 63764
Telephone: (314) 238-2010

Maternity Center Association
48 East 92nd Street
New York, NY 10028
Telephone: (212) 369-7300

For Further Reading

Bowe-Gutman, Sonia. *Teen Pregnancy.*
Minneapolis, MN: Lerner Publications
Company, 1987, 72 pages. This book discusses
the problems of teen pregnancy, the choices a
pregnant teen can make, and how pregnant
teens can get help.

Folkenberg, J. "Teen Pregnancy: Who Opts for
Adoption?" *Psychology Today*, May 1985, page
16. (A) This article discusses the reasons teens
decide to give up their babies for adoption.

Kantrowitz, B. "Teenagers and Abortion."
Newsweek, October 12, 1987, page 81. (A)
This article discusses teens who decide to end
their pregnancies.

Raible, H. "Parents Too Soon: The Problems of
Teenage Parenthood." *Choices*, March 1987,
pages 6–7 + . This article discusses teen
couples trying to cope with having babies.

Stark, E. "Young, Innocent and Pregnant."
Psychology Today, October 1986, pages 28–
30 + . (A) This article discusses the problems
of pregnant young teenagers.

"Why It's So Hard to Be a Teenage Parent."
Choices, May 1987, page 23. This article
discusses the problems teenage parents often
have after they decide to keep their babies.

Index

About the Author
Tracy Hughes has been both an elementary school teacher and a
counselor to pregnant teenagers. A graduate of Wesleyan University,
Ms. Hughes is now completing graduate work in the social services
field.

About the Editor
Evan Stark is a well-known sociologist, educator, and therapist
as well as a popular lecturer on women's and children's health issues.
Dr. Stark was the Henry Rutgers Fellow at Rutgers University, an as-
sociate at the Institution for Social and Policy Studies at Yale University, and a Fulbright Fellow at the University of Essex. He is the author
of many publications in the field of family relations and is the father of
four children.

Acknowledgments and Photo Credits
P. 18, 21, 30, 40, 41, 45, Stuart Rabinowitz; p. 2, 15, 24, 48, 57, Blackbirch
Graphics, Inc.; p. 11, 33, 34, 37; Sonja Kalter

Design/Production: Blackbirch Graphics, Inc.
Cover Photograph: Stuart Rabinowitz